CHAPTER 1

THE SOUTH SECEDES

For decades the arguments about **slavery** have been growing louder between people who live in the **Northern states** and people who live in the **Southern states**. Northerners believe slavery should be **abolished for moral reasons**. Southerners feel the **end of slavery will destroy their region's rural economy**. Many in the South think the election of Northerner **Abraham Lincoln** to be president of the United States will be a serious blow to their way of life. But what will they do about it?

WHO WERE THE SOUTHERN PLANTERS?

THE ECONOMY IN THE **NORTHERN** PART OF THE UNITED STATES IS USING MORE AND MORE **FACTORIES** IN THE EARLY 1800s.

THE ECONOMY IN THE **SOUTHERN** PART IS STILL BASED ON **AGRICULTURE** (FARMING).

MANY SOUTHERN PLANTATIONS ARE LIKE "BRANDON" ON THE JAMES RIVER IN VIRGINIA. WILLIAM BYRD HARRISON FINISHES A NEW HOUSE THERE IN 1825.

Martha Southern Stewart's Mansions

MY MANSION HAS INDOOR BATHROOMS! EACH FLOOR IS 3,756 SQUARE FEET!

HARRISON USES HUNDREDS OF **SLAVE** WORKERS TO GROW HIS CROPS. SOUTHERNERS BELIEVE THAT ENDING SLAVERY WOULD DESTROY THEIR REGION'S ECONOMY.

HI, EDMUND RUFFIN!

HARRISON!! HAVE YOU READ THE LATEST FROM THAT NORTHERN MANIAC, **WILLIAM LLOYD GARRISON**, IN "THE LIBERATOR"?

FREEDOM SOUTH

CALM DOWN. HE CAN'T **ABOLISH** SLAVERY.

THOSE YANKEES WILL KEEP SLAVERY OUT OF NEW STATES — THEN TRY TO END IT HERE! **I'LL FIGHT THEM!**

:SIGH: THERE GOES MY AGITATOR NEIGHBOR.

AND THE MAN WHO WILL FIRE THE FIRST SHOT OF **THE CIVIL WAR** next!

HOW DID THE SOUTH'S SECESSION BEGIN?

AMERICANS HAVE ARGUED FOR DECADES ABOUT WHETHER SLAVERY SHOULD BE LEGAL OR NOT. THIS DEBATE SPLINTERS THE NATION IN THE **PRESIDENTIAL ELECTION OF 1860**...

DON'T WORRY. I WAS FAIRLY ELECTED. I WILL HOLD THE NATION TOGETHER.

THAT WILL BE HARD TO DO, **ABRAHAM LINCOLN.** LOOK AT HOW THE UNITED STATES VOTERS SPLIT AMONG FOUR PRESIDENTIAL CANDIDATES! **TIME IS RUNNING OUT!**

TIK TIK TIK

ELECTORAL VOTES

- LINCOLN (REPUBLICAN)
- BRECKINRIDGE (SOUTHERN DEMOCRAT)
- DOUGLAS (NORTHERN DEMOCRAT)
- BELL (CONSTITUTION UNION)

BOYD '03

THE SOUTH

HAS HAD SLAVERY FOR 200 YEARS! NORTHERN VOTERS ELECTED LINCOLN TO ATTACK OUR WAY OF LIFE!! HE IS NOT THE U.S. PRESIDENT — HE IS THE **NORTHERN** PRESIDENT.

INSIDE SCOOP: SOME SOUTHERN VOTERS *COULDN'T* PICK LINCOLN. ALABAMA DID NOT PUT HIS NAME ON ITS BALLOT!

ANGRY "FIRE-EATER" POLITICIANS OF SOUTH CAROLINA CALL A MEETING.

Constitution

SOUTH CAROLINA ALMOST LEFT THE UNITED STATES IN 1850. NOW WE **MUST** LEAVE TO **SAVE SLAVERY!!**

ON DEC. 20, 1860, THESE DELEGATES VOTE 169-0 TO SECEDE (LEAVE) FROM THE U.S.

OUR **STATE'S RIGHTS** ARE MORE IMPORTANT THAN NATIONAL LAWS. WE WILL MAKE CAROLINA A SEPARATE REPUBLIC!

next: **FALLING DOMINOES**

WHAT WERE THE 1ST CONFEDERATE STATES?

IT LOOKS LIKE A WAVE OF TROUBLE IS BUILDING IN **1861** FOR THE NEW PRESIDENT OF THE UNITED STATES, **ABRAHAM LINCOLN**! AFTER SOUTH CAROLINA, SIX MORE SOUTHERN STATES VOTE TO SECEDE (LEAVE) FROM THE U.S.

MISSISSIPPI	FLORIDA	ALABAMA	GEORGIA	LOUISIANA	TEXAS
JANUARY 9, 1861	JANUARY 10	JANUARY 11	JANUARY 19	JANUARY 26	FEBRUARY 1

United States Constitution

SECESSION NOW!

SECESSION TOMORROW!

SECESSION FOREVER!!

BALLOT
☐ WE STAY
☐ WE GO

SOUTHERN POLITICIANS ARE MAKING THESE DECISIONS TO LEAVE. BUT **NOT ALL** SOUTHERNERS WANT TO SPLIT.

Tik Tik Tik Tok Tik...

ALABAMA'S POLITICIANS SPLIT IN THEIR VOTE TO SECEDE: 61-39.

MAYBE WE CAN WORK WITH LINCOLN. LET'S TRY TO PASS A FEDERAL SLAVE CODE FOR AMERICA'S WESTERN TERRITORIES.

NO!

SOME SUGGEST EACH VOTER GET A SAY ABOUT SECESSION. THE PRO-SLAVERY LOUISIANA POLITICIANS REFUSE TO HOLD A STATE-WIDE VOTE.

THESE SEVEN SOUTHERN STATES MAKE A NEW GOVERNMENT: "**THE CONFEDERATE STATES OF AMERICA**." IN FEBRUARY THEIR POLITICIANS WRITE A CONSTITUTION THAT INCLUDES THESE IDEAS:

WE WILL NOT "PROMOTE THE GENERAL WELFARE." EACH STATE IS INDEPENDENT OF THE OTHER STATES.

SLAVERY IS GUARANTEED IN ALL OUR STATES.

THE CONFEDERATE CONGRESS MAY NOT TAX STATES TO PAY FOR ROADS AND CANALS.

THE PRESIDENT MAY SERVE ONLY ONE SIX-YEAR TERM, BUT HE GETS A LINE-ITEM VETO OVER THE BUDGET.

...AND OUR PRESIDENT IS JEFFERSON DAVIS!

BOYD '03

next: **THE BORDER**

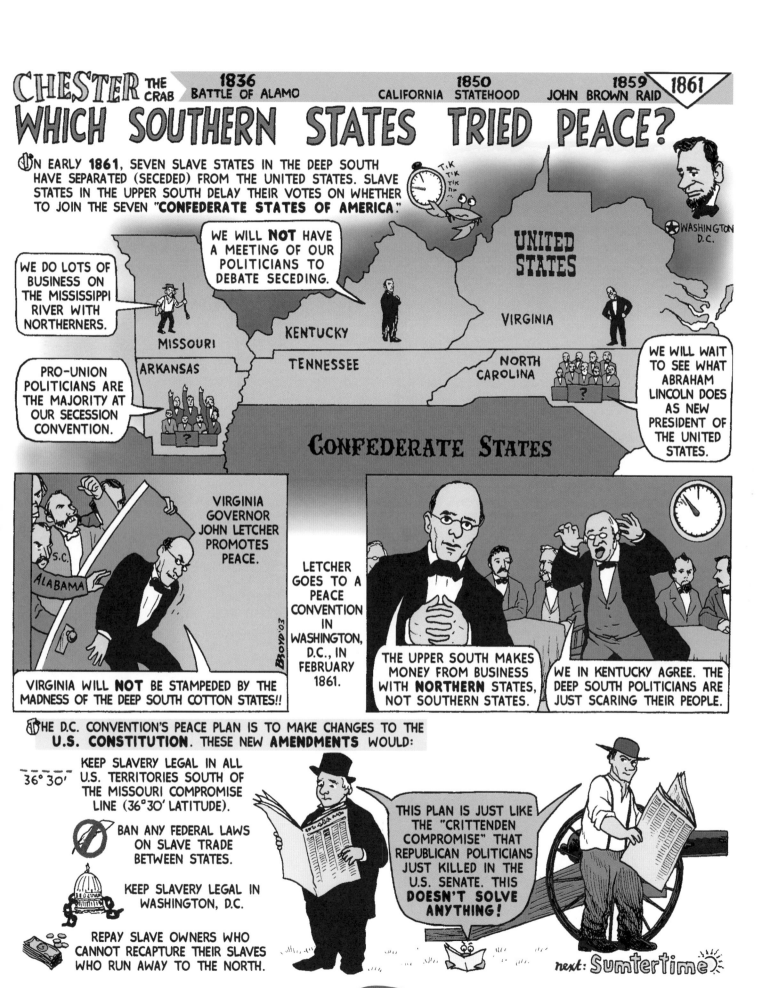

CHESTER THE CRAB

1836	1850	1859	1861
BATTLE OF ALAMO	CALIFORNIA STATEHOOD	JOHN BROWN RAID	

WHY WAS FORT SUMTER IMPORTANT IN 1861?

ABRAHAM **LINCOLN** IS SWORN IN AS PRESIDENT OF THE UNITED STATES ON **MARCH 4, 1861.**

I PROMISE TWO THINGS:
1. THE FEDERAL GOVERNMENT WILL AVOID VIOLENCE — UNLESS IT IS FORCED ON US.
2. WE WILL HOLD ON TO THE FORTS AND PLACES THAT BELONG TO THE FEDERAL GOVERNMENT.

NORTHERN STATES AND SOUTHERN STATES ARE **NOT** ENEMIES. WE ARE FRIENDS. WE WILL ALL SEE THAT AGAIN WHEN WE ARE TOUCHED BY THE BETTER ANGELS OF OUR NATURE.

REACTION TO LINCOLN'S SPEECH IS MIXED. IN **SOUTH CAROLINA** . . .

THAT ORANGUTAN IN THE WHITE HOUSE JUST DECLARED BATTLE!!

WHILE IN **VIRGINIA** . . .

OUR STATE MUST CHOOSE BETWEEN INVASION BY THE NORTHERN ARMY OR INVASION BY THE CONFEDERATE ARMY.

NORTH

SOUTH

FT. SUMTER IN THE HARBOR OF CHARLESTON, SOUTH CAROLINA, SAYS SUPPLIES WILL RUN OUT IN SIX WEEKS IF WE DON'T SEND HELP.

A VIRGINIAN MEETS SECRETLY WITH LINCOLN IN EARLY APRIL. LINCOLN TELLS HIM:

OK, IF VIRGINIA STAYS IN THE U.S., I'LL GIVE UP FORT SUMTER. GETTING A STATE FOR A FORT IS NO BAD BUSINESS.

VIRGINIA'S POLITICIANS DO NOT ANSWER LINCOLN'S OFFER.

I HAVE NO CHOICE, THEN. RESUPPLY FORT SUMTER.

EDMUND RUFFIN OF VIRGINIA FIRES THE FIRST CONFEDERATE CANNON SHOT AT THE FORT ON **APRIL 12, 1861.** THE BOMBARDMENT KEEPS THE U.S. NAVY SHIPS AWAY FROM THE FORT.

OK! OK! WE SURRENDER!

next: Breakaway Republics

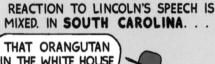

THE FIRST FIGHTS

United States President Abraham Lincoln is determined to **preserve the Union** by force if necessary. Early on, both sides try to **capture the others' capital city**. That makes the Virginia landscape between **Richmond** and **Washington, D.C.**, into the battleground. Non-soldiers quickly get caught in the middle . . .

WHO WON THE 1ST CIVIL WAR BATTLE?

UNITED STATES PRESIDENT **ABRAHAM LINCOLN:**

THE UNITED STATES IS **ONE NATION** THAT CAN'T BE DIVIDED. I WILL PRESERVE THE UNION BY FORCE IF NECESSARY.

LINCOLN'S FIRST PROBLEM: MORE THAN HALF OF THE U.S. ARMY'S OFFICERS QUIT TO JOIN THEIR HOME STATES IN THE CONFEDERACY. TWO ARE **ROBERT E. LEE** AND **J.E.B. STUART.**

STUART JOINS THOMAS JACKSON'S FORCE DEFENDING VIRGINIA NEAR WASHINGTON, D.C. THEY CLASH WITH UNION TROOPS ON JULY 21, 1861. "**THE FIRST BATTLE OF MANASSAS (BULL RUN)**" WAS THE FIRST MAJOR BATTLE OF THE CIVIL WAR.

THE.. THE YANKEES HAVE CROSSED BULL RUN! **WE GOTTA GO!**

THERE STANDS JACKSON LIKE A **STONE WALL!** .. RALLY BEHIND THE VIRGINIANS!!

ABOUT 37,000 UNION TROOPS ALMOST SWEEP 32,000 CONFEDERATE TROOPS FROM THE OPEN FIELDS NEAR THE MANASSAS RAILROAD JUNCTION. BUT JACKSON'S MEN HOLD THE SOUTHERN LINE AND TURN BACK THE ATTACK.

UNION TROOPS OVERRUN PEOPLE WHO CAME FROM WASHINGTON TO PICNIC AND WATCH THE BATTLE. THE RETREAT BECOMES A PANIC. THIS BATTLE CONVINCES NORTHERNERS THE WAR WILL BE LONG AND DIFFICULT.

next: **WAR BAND**

WHO WAS IN THE "CONTRABAND"?

WITH THE START OF THE CIVIL WAR, THE SMALL VIRGINIA TOWN OF HAMPTON BECOMES LIKE A BULLSEYE.

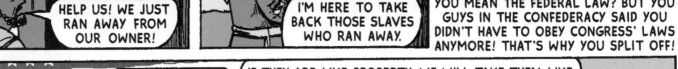

WHO BURNED HAMPTON IN THE WAR?

BY JULY **1861**, MORE THAN 900 SLAVES HAVE ESCAPED INTO UNION-HELD FORT MONROE.

IT LOOKS LIKE MOST OF THEM ARE WOMEN AND CHILDREN.

WHAT WILL YOU DO IN THERE?

DON'T KNOW. BUT I NEED HOUSING, CLOTHING, FOOD, AND A JOB!

HMMM. WITH WHITES GOING WEST AND BLACKS TO THE FORT, HAMPTON IS AS EMPTY AS A CHURCH ON FRIDAY NIGHT.

EXCEPT FOR **THOSE** GUYS.

GRRR— WE CAN'T BEAT THE YANKS OUT OF FORT MONROE.

THEY WILL MAKE **OUR** HOMES A BIG CAMP FOR THOSE SLAVES!

WELL IF **WE** CAN'T HAVE HAMPTON, **THEY** CAN'T HAVE IT EITHER!!

ON AUG. 7, 1861, SOUTHERN SOLDIERS SET FIRE TO HAMPTON. THEY BURN 130 EMPTY HOMES AND STORES. THIS SURPRISES NORTHERNERS.

HAMPTON'S BURNING IS THE FIRST SIGN THE CIVIL WAR WILL BE BAD FOR NON-SOLDIERS TOO. THE WAR WILL DAMAGE A LOT OF PROPERTY.

next: **100,000 SOLDIERS**

WHEN WAS THE 1ST ATTACK ON RICHMOND?

Ⓐ **A**FTER SOUTHERNERS BURN HAMPTON, MANY ESCAPED SLAVES BUILD SHACKS NEXT TO THE CHIMNEYS OF THE BURNED HOUSES. FINDING SHELTER FOR ALL THE ESCAPED SLAVES IS HARD.

ESPECIALLY WHEN THE UNION ARMY SHOWS UP.

MOVE. WE NEED ROOMS FOR **100,000** SOLDIERS!

I GET SHELTER AND FOOD IF I SHOW GENERAL GEORGE McCLELLAN THE BEST WAY TO RICHMOND.

WHY RICHMOND?

VIRGINIA IS A BIG BATTLEGROUND BECAUSE **RICHMOND** IS THE **CAPITAL OF THE CONFEDERACY**.

Ⓑ **O**N MAY 1862 McCLELLAN SENDS HIS ARMY UP THE PENINSULA. CONFEDERATES SLOW HIM DOWN IN THE BATTLE OF WILLIAMSBURG.

THIS BATTLE ON MAY 5, **1862**, SHOWS THAT SOLDIERS ON HORSES (**"CAVALRY"**) CAN PLUG HOLES IN BATTLELINES DURING A FIGHT.

HOLD! STOP THE YANKEES HERE SO OUR ARMY CAN GET BACK TO RICHMOND!!

THEN McCLELLAN LOSES "THE SEVEN DAYS BATTLE" AND RETREATS FROM RICHMOND.

Grrrr ...WE'LL BE BACK!

STILL, WHEREVER UNION TROOPS GO, THEY FREE SLAVES. MANY FREED PEOPLE MOVE TO HAMPTON. BY DECEMBER 1863, ABOUT 10,000 SUCH REFUGEES ARE ON THE LOWER PENINSULA. SOME LIVE IN TOBACCO BARNS WITH "ROOMS" MARKED IN CHALK.

HEY, GET YOUR CLAW BACK ON YOUR SIDE! END

IRON GIANTS

United States President Abraham Lincoln uses the large Union navy to **blockade Southern ports** from receiving supplies from Europe. The Confederacy must break through this barrier of wooden warships. Would an **iron ship** work?

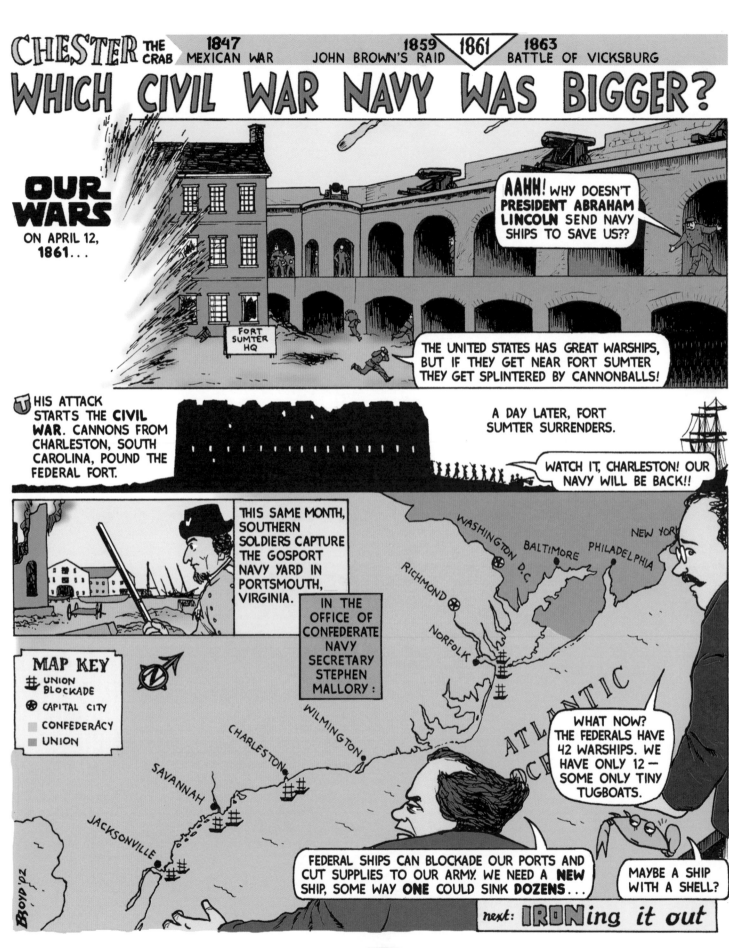

WHICH CIVIL WAR NAVY WAS BIGGER?

OUR WARS

ON APRIL 12, 1861...

AAHH! WHY DOESN'T PRESIDENT ABRAHAM LINCOLN SEND NAVY SHIPS TO SAVE US??

FORT SUMTER HQ

THE UNITED STATES HAS GREAT WARSHIPS, BUT IF THEY GET NEAR FORT SUMTER THEY GET SPLINTERED BY CANNONBALLS!

THIS ATTACK STARTS THE **CIVIL WAR.** CANNONS FROM CHARLESTON, SOUTH CAROLINA, POUND THE FEDERAL FORT.

A DAY LATER, FORT SUMTER SURRENDERS.

WATCH IT, CHARLESTON! OUR NAVY WILL BE BACK!!

THIS SAME MONTH, SOUTHERN SOLDIERS CAPTURE THE GOSPORT NAVY YARD IN PORTSMOUTH, VIRGINIA.

IN THE OFFICE OF CONFEDERATE NAVY SECRETARY STEPHEN MALLORY:

WASHINGTON D.C.
BALTIMORE
PHILADELPHIA
NEW YORK
RICHMOND
NORFOLK

MAP KEY
⚓ UNION BLOCKADE
✪ CAPITAL CITY
☐ CONFEDERACY
☐ UNION

WILMINGTON
CHARLESTON
SAVANNAH
JACKSONVILLE

ATLANTIC OCEAN

WHAT NOW? THE FEDERALS HAVE 42 WARSHIPS. WE HAVE ONLY 12 — SOME ONLY TINY TUGBOATS.

FEDERAL SHIPS CAN BLOCKADE OUR PORTS AND CUT SUPPLIES TO OUR ARMY. WE NEED A **NEW** SHIP, SOME WAY **ONE** COULD SINK **DOZENS**...

MAYBE A SHIP WITH A SHELL?

BOYD pz

next: **IRON**ing *it out*

HOW DID THE SOUTH MAKE THE VIRGINIA?

DURING THE **CIVIL WAR,** CONFEDERATE NAVY SECRETARY STEPHEN MALLORY VISITS THE TREDEGAR IRON WORKS IN RICHMOND, VIRGINIA . . .

THE NORTH HAS DOZENS OF WOODEN WARSHIPS. WE CANNOT BUILD THAT MANY. WHAT IF WE BUILD **ONE** THAT COULDN'T BE SUNK? ONE OF IRON?!

WHAT IF PIGS COULD **FLY?!** WE CAN'T MAKE ARMOR THICKER THAN ONE INCH WITHOUT BIG CHANGES TO OUR MACHINERY!!

NEXT MALLORY VISITS THE GOSPORT NAVY YARD IN PORTSMOUTH, VIRGINIA.

DO YOU HAVE ANY WOODEN SHIPS WE COULD JUST ADD METAL ARMOR TO?

THE YANKEES SCUTTLED THAT FRIGATE, THE MERRIMACK. ITS STEAM ENGINES ARE WATERLOGGED, BUT WE CAN TRY IT.

WHERE WOULD WE GET IRON?

TAKE MINE!

THE CONFEDERATES TEAR UP RAILROAD TRACK TO GET ENOUGH IRON TO COVER THE MERRIMACK.

I'VE BEEN WRECKING ON THE RAILROAD . . .

THE SHIP IS COVERED, REFLOATED, AND RENAMED THE **CSS VIRGINIA** ON FEB. 17, 1862.

NINE MONTHS OF CONSTRUCTION MADE A MIRACLE!!

NOW ALL YOU NEED IS A STEEL MAGNOLIA!

NORTHERN SPIES HAVE BEEN WATCHING THIS WORK.

HMM. I HOPE THE UNION IRONCLAD SHIP UP IN NEW YORK IS READY TO FIGHT THIS **MONSTER!**

next: **MONITOR DUTY**

WHO BUILT THE NORTH'S IRONCLAD?

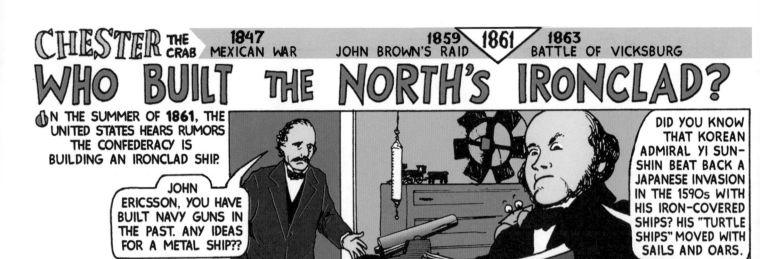

IN THE SUMMER OF **1861**, THE UNITED STATES HEARS RUMORS THE CONFEDERACY IS BUILDING AN IRONCLAD SHIP.

JOHN ERICSSON, YOU HAVE BUILT NAVY GUNS IN THE PAST. ANY IDEAS FOR A METAL SHIP??

DID YOU KNOW THAT KOREAN ADMIRAL YI SUN-SHIN BEAT BACK A JAPANESE INVASION IN THE 1590s WITH HIS IRON-COVERED SHIPS? HIS "TURTLE SHIPS" MOVED WITH SAILS AND OARS.

WHO CARES ABOUT KOREAN SHIPS?!!

WELL HOW ABOUT THIS? I DESIGNED THIS MODEL OF A FLOATING CANNON A FEW YEARS AGO.

THE U.S. NAVY TELLS ERICSSON TO BUILD THIS SHIP IN 100 DAYS. THEN THEY PESTER HIM...

IT WILL SINK WHEN YOU LAUNCH, RIGHT?

WHAT KIND OF ENGINE?

WHAT IF THE GUN FAILS?

HOW WILL IT GO TO SEA?

HE IS THE **TRUE** IRONCLAD!

ERICSSON'S DESIGN IS STRANGE:

HIS SHIP'S GUN TURRET TURNS TO FIRE IN ANY DIRECTION!

IT IS AMAZING FOR WHAT IT DOES **NOT** HAVE ABOVE WATER: NO SMOKESTACK, NO PADDLEWHEEL, NO SAILS!

PILOT HOUSE, FOR STEERING

BECAUSE THE CREW WORKS BELOW THE WATER, THERE IS A NEW KIND OF TOILET AND A FAN-POWERED AIR SYSTEM!

TO PROVE THE WORRIERS WRONG, ERICSSON STANDS ON THE DECK OF THE **USS MONITOR** AS IT LAUNCHES IN NEW YORK ON JAN. 30, 1862.

WOW! IT'S **NOT** AN IRON COFFIN!

next:
IRON FIST

WHO WON THE BATTLE OF THE IRONCLADS?

THE UNITED STATES NAVY'S **FIRST IRONCLAD** SHIP COMES TO HAMPTON ROADS ON MARCH 8, **1862**. THE **USS MONITOR** FINDS CHAOS. THE USS MINNESOTA IS STUCK AFTER THE DAY'S BATTLE WITH THE CONFEDERATE IRONCLAD, CSS VIRGINIA.

GO! GO!

GET US OUT OF HERE!!

DON'T WORRY! WE ARE HERE TO DEFEND YOU IF THE SOUTHERN IRONCLAD COMES BACK.

YOU?!! A CHEESEBOX ON A RAFT?

THE NEXT MORNING, MARCH 9, THE VIRGINIA RETURNS TO FINISH OFF THE WOODEN FLEET.

BLAM

HEY, WHAT IS THAT COMING FROM BEHIND THE MINNESOTA? A FLOATING WATER TANK?

FWOOM

BOYD '02

THE TWO IRON SHIPS TRADE SHELLS FOR FOUR HOURS!

WE'RE HIT!!

THEY CAN'T HURT US! OUR ARMOR IS 8 INCHES THICK!

NEITHER SHIP CAN HURT THE OTHER — EVEN WHEN THE VIRGINIA GETS STUCK ON A SHOAL.

MORE POWER TO THE BOILERS! GET US OFF THIS SAND!!

THE VIRGINIA GETS FREE AND TRIES TO RAM THE MONITOR. THE MONITOR IS TOO FAST FOR IT. AS THE TIDE FALLS, THE VIRGINIA HEADS BACK TO PORT IN PORTSMOUTH, VIRGINIA.

THE BATTLE OF THE IRONCLADS IS A DRAW. THE TWO SHIPS DON'T FIGHT AGAIN, BUT THEY HAVE PROVEN THE AGE OF WOODEN WARSHIPS IS OVER!

END

CHAPTER 4

TERRIBLE ANTIETAM

Confederate General Robert E. Lee believes he can put pressure on the **Union capital of Washington, D.C.**, by crossing to the north side of the **Potomac River**. Plus, an invasion of **Maryland** may make people there who support the Southern cause feel bold enough to **secede** from the Union. Lee can put the war permanently on Northern soil. But what is that piece of paper lying there in the grass?

WHY WAS THERE A BATTLE AT ANTIETAM?

NORTHERN SOLDIERS FIGHT SOUTHERN SOLDIERS IN AUGUST 1862 IN NORTHERN VIRGINIA...

GENERAL ROBERT E. LEE! WE HAVE BEATEN THE UNION ARMY AT THE SECOND BATTLE OF MANASSAS — JUST LIKE WE DID A YEAR AGO AT THE FIRST BATTLE OF MANASSAS!

LET'S GO TO DISNEY WORLD!

NO, WE'RE GOING TO ATTACK SOME MORE.

WHILE UNION TROOPS REST IN WASHINGTON, D.C., WE MOVE INTO **MARYLAND.**

THIS WILL PUSH THE FIGHTING AWAY FROM VIRGINIA'S FARMS AT HARVEST TIME. MAYBE WE CAN ALSO CONVINCE MARYLANDERS TO SECEDE FROM, OR LEAVE, THE UNITED STATES.

(MARYLAND WAS A SLAVE STATE BEFORE THE WAR.)

Map labels: PHILADELPHIA, HARRISBURG, Pennsylvania, Maryland, BALTIMORE, APPALACHIAN MOUNTAINS, HARPERS FERRY, WINCHESTER, WASHINGTON D.C., LEESBURG, POTOMAC RIVER, Virginia

LEE'S CONFEDERATE ARMY MOVES TO FREDERICK, MARYLAND, IN EARLY SEPTEMBER.

MERRY MARYLANDERS! THE SOUTH WISHES TO HELP YOU THROW OFF THE FOREIGN GOVERNMENT OF ABE LINCOLN!

THESE RAGAMUFFINS ARE SO... DIRTY! I DON'T THINK THE WHOLE POTOMAC RIVER COULD WASH THEM CLEAN!

UNION SOLDIERS FOLLOW LEE.

OK, GUYS, WE'LL REST HERE.

HEY — THAT LOOKS LIKE SOME ... PAPERS?

BOYD '04

next: **My Side of the Mountain**

WHAT DID STUART TELL LEE IN MARYLAND?

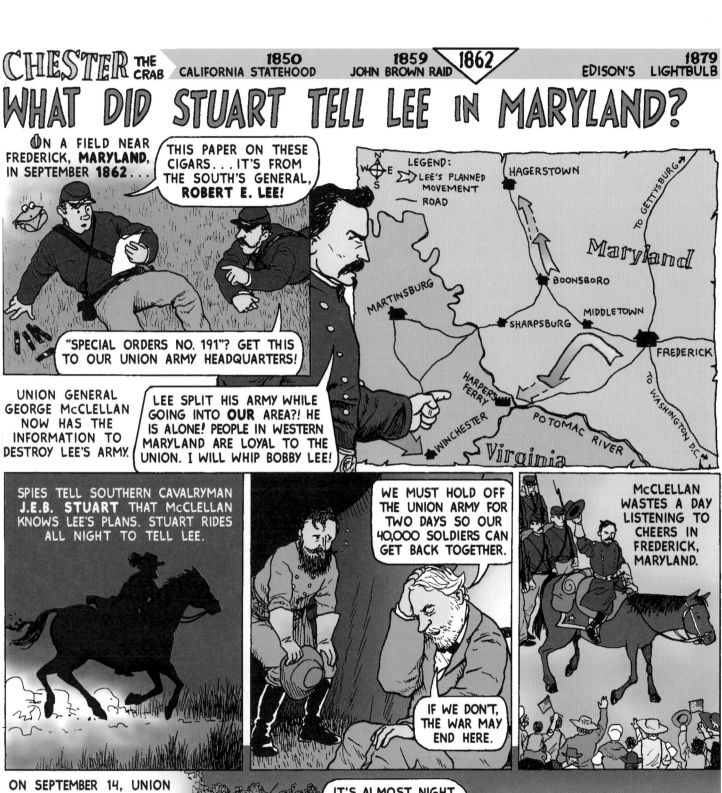

HOW DID THE BATTLE OF ANTIETAM START?

ON SEPT. 16, **1862**, THE BIG UNION ARMY SETS UP NEAR THE CONFEDERATE ARMY EAST OF SHARPSBURG, **MARYLAND.**

GENERAL GEORGE McCLELLAN!! WE HAVE 70,000 MEN READY TO ATTACK! *LET'S GO!*

NO, NO— **ROBERT E. LEE** IS TRICKY. WE MUST BE CAREFUL.

GENERAL LEE, I BRING YOU MORE MEN AND THE GUNS WE TOOK FROM THE UNION FORT AT HARPERS FERRY YESTERDAY.

GOOD JOB, **STONEWALL JACKSON.** YOU GOT HERE JUST IN TIME!

THE NEXT DAY, **SEPT. 17, 1862,** THE FEDERAL TROOPS ATTACK. THEY PUSH THROUGH A CORNFIELD NORTH OF SHARPSBURG. STONEWALL JACKSON'S TROOPS DEFEND DUNKER CHURCH.

YIKES! I'VE NEVER SEEN RAIN FALL FASTER THAN THE BULLETS ARE FLYING AROUND US!

BOYD '04

AFTER TWO HOURS OF FIGHTING, UNION SOLDIERS ALMOST TAKE DUNKER CHURCH.

WE'RE ALMOST OUT OF AMMO!

THEN FIX YOUR BAYONETS! WE HAVE POURED OUT OUR BLOOD LIKE WATER TO TAKE THAT CHURCH!

RESTED CONFEDERATES PUSH THE UNION TROOPS BACK TO WHERE THEY HAD BEEN AT THE START OF BATTLE. THE COST IS HIGH.

HOOD! I WANT TO CONGRATULATE YOUR MEN. WHERE ARE THEY?

DEAD ON THE FIELD.

next: no sunken garden

WHO WON ANTIETAM CREEK's BRIDGE?

CONFEDERATE AND UNION TROOPS FIGHT IN **MARYLAND** ON SEPT. 17, **1862**...

WE HAD TO SEND MEN TO PROTECT DUNKER CHURCH NORTH OF HERE. YOU 2,500 BOYS ARE ALL WE HAVE TO HOLD THE CENTER OF OUR DEFENSIVE LINE.

GENERAL LEE, WE WILL STAY IN THIS SUNKEN LANE UNTIL THE SUN GOES DOWN OR VICTORY IS WON!

THESE CONFEDERATES WAIT UNTIL THE NEAT LINES OF FEDERALS ARE ALMOST IN THE LANE, **THEN**...

AFTER THREE HOURS OF BRUTAL FIGHTING, UNION SOLDIERS GET INTO ONE END OF THE TRENCH. SUDDENLY THE PROTECTING WALLS BECOME AN OPEN GRAVE.

THIS IS NOW NICKNAMED "THE BLOODY LANE."

LATE THAT MORNING, YANKS ON THE SOUTH END OF THE BATTLEFIELD BEGIN ATTACKING.

IF WE TAKE THAT BRIDGE OVER **ANTIETAM CREEK**, WE CAN PUSH THE REBELS OUT OF SHARPSBURG AND INTO THE **POTOMAC RIVER!**

ONLY 520 CONFEDERATES ARE ON A STEEP HILL OVER THE BRIDGE. THEY CUT DOWN SEVERAL UNION CHARGES ON THE NARROW BRIDGE.

ONLY WHEN THE CONFEDERATES RUN OUT OF AMMUNITION DO UNION MEN CROSS THE BRIDGE.

I NEED BACKUP!! WHERE CAN I FIND MORE MEN?

next: Emancipation Nation

INDEX

MEET THE AUTHOR

Bentley Boyd drew Chester the Crab's tales for the <u>Daily Press</u> of Newport News, Virginia, from 1995 to 2008. He also drew elephants and donkeys as a political cartoonist, and long ago in his own classes he drew his teachers (none of them as elephants or donkeys or crabs). Bentley did not study art, he studied History and Literature at Harvard University. Bentley lives in Williamsburg, Virginia, with his two sons, Samuel and Truman – who love *Star Wars* even more than he does and can sometimes be found wandering with him in another century . . .

OTHER TITLES IN THIS SERIES:

Put Chester Comix **EXPANDED ADVENTURES** on your iTouch, iPhone or iPad!

Available on the App Store

FREE teacher's guides and sample pages and Bentley's Blog at WWW.CHESTERCOMIX.COM